AMERICAN MUSEUM OF NATURAL HISTORY

The Exquisite Butterfly Companion

Hazel Davies

Sterling Signature
NEW YORK

STERLING SIGNATURE and the distinctive Sterling Signature logo
are trademarks of Sterling Publishing Co., Inc.

10 9 8 7 6 5 4 3 2 1

Published by Sterling Publishing Co., Inc.
387 Park Avenue South, New York, NY 10016
© 2011 by Sterling Publishing Co., Inc.

Text by Hazel Davies
Paper crafts by Michael Flannery

Distributed in Canada by Sterling Publishing
C/o Canadian Manda Group, 165 Dufferin Street
Toronto, Ontario, Canada M6K 3H6
Distributed in the United Kingdom by GMC Distribution Services
Castle Place, 166 High Street, Lewes, East Sussex, England BN7 1XU
Distributed in Australia by Capricorn Link (Australia) Pty. Ltd.
P.O. Box 704, Windsor, NSW 2756, Australia

This book is part of the *American Museum of Natural History Exquisite Butterfly Companion*
book and kit and is not to be sold separately.

Sterling ISBN 978-1-4027-7875-9

For information about custom editions, special sales, premium and
corporate purchases, please contact Sterling Special Sales Department
at 800-805-5489 or specialsales@sterlingpublishing.com.

Contents

Introduction

BUTTERFLIES AND MOTHS have fascinated people for centuries. Their bright colors, varied wing shapes, and endless patterns capture the imagination; they are the stuff of myth and folklore. The ancient Greek word for butterfly is *psuche*, which in English translates to "psyche" or "soul"—and indeed butterflies are spiritual symbols in many cultures. In the Middle Ages they were thought to be fairies intent on stealing milk and butter. The Old English name *buttorfleoge* comes from the words for "butter" and "fly," which perhaps arose from that notion and eventually led to the modern term butterfly. Or the name may have simply come from the many yellow sulphur butterflies (family Pieridae) seen flying in the spring that looked like butter-colored flies.

Butterfly collecting was a very popular pastime in Europe during the 1800s. People of all classes joined societies and attended field trips in pursuit of knowledge and specimens. Wealthy people, with both the time and money to indulge their obsession, were able to accumulate huge collections by employing professional collectors and funding expeditions to capture exotic specimens in far-off lands. Lionel Walter Rothschild (later to become Lord Rothschild) was born into a distinguished banking family, but his real passion lay in natural history. In 1892, he opened his own museum in Tring, England, which housed the largest private zoological collection in the world—including 2.25 million butterflies and moths. Rothschild's specimens now form the core of the collection at the Natural History Museum, London.

More recently, butterfly watching, or "butterflying," has become a popular hobby with numerous clubs and festivals devoted to the activity. People equipped with binoculars, field guides, and cameras (to collect photographs rather than specimens)

A sulphur butterfly (*Phoebis philea*)

make regular field trips in search of species on their checklists. Tour companies lead butterfly-focused trips to hotspots like Costa Rica and the Amazon. But you don't need to travel far from home to enjoy these wonderfully dazzling creatures. As more and more butterfly conservatories open around the world, exotic species are practically being brought to your doorstep.

Butterfly and Moth Basics

What Are Butterflies and Moths?

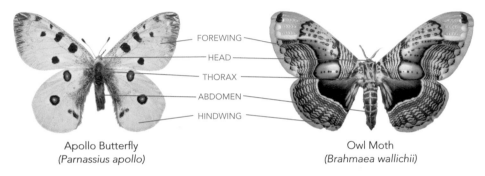

Apollo Butterfly
(*Parnassius apollo*)

Owl Moth
(*Brahmaea wallichii*)

BUTTERFLIES AND MOTHS are insects, and like all insects, their bodies consist of three major segments: a head, a thorax, and an abdomen. They have six jointed legs and four wings attached to the thorax. The soft body is encased in an exoskeleton made of a horny polysaccharide material called chitin. What makes butterflies and moths unique among insects are the scales that cover their wings and bodies. Scales are modified hairs that form an overlapping pattern on the wings like a tiled roof. Each scale is a single color. The colors may result from internal pigments, or they may be due to a specialized surface structure on the scale, reflecting the light we see thus giving the wings a shiny, iridescent quality.

Butterfly wing scales at
100x magnification

ABDOMEN

SPIRACLES

Butterflies and moths do not have a closed circulation system of veins and arteries like humans; instead, a liquid called hemolymph fills the body cavity and is moved around by a tubular heart. A simple nervous system runs throughout the entire body and controls motion, digestion, circulation of hemolymph, and reproduction. There are no lungs in butterflies and moths; they breathe through holes in their exoskeleton called spiracles. Each body segment bears a pair of spiracles—one on each side of the body—that look like tiny pores along the side of the thorax and abdomen. The spiracles connect to a network of tracheae that distribute oxygen throughout the body.

Insects are ectothermic, or cold-blooded; they cannot maintain a constant body temperature on their own. Since butterflies need a body temperature between 77–111 degrees Fahrenheit (25–44 degrees Celsius) to be able to fly, they warm up their flight muscles by basking with their wings outstretched in a sunny spot. Their wings absorb heat and radiate it into the air around their bodies. If a butterfly gets too hot, it finds a shady area or folds its wings closed and stands with them parallel to the sun's rays. Moths cannot bask at night, so instead they appear to shiver. In actuality, they are vibrating their flight muscles to generate heat.

Just like humans, butterflies and moths experience the world around them through five senses. They see through compound eyes made up of thousands of individual facets, called ommatidia, which can detect motion very well and see a wide spectrum of colors, including ultraviolet. But their eyes do not focus clearly, and they cannot see details from a distance.

A simple membrane that acts like an eardrum by detecting vibrations is found in many species of moths and some butterflies. Moths flying at night use this eardrum to detect the echolocation cries of predatory bats. Male Cracker butterflies (*Hamadryas* spp.) can communicate with one another through a surprisingly loud cracking sound made by their wings, which is thought to be a territorial warning.

ANTENNA

PROBOSCIS

Butterflies and moths detect odors through chemoreceptors located on their antennae. These sense organs are very powerful; some male moths can detect the scent, or pheromone, of a female moth from a distance of over a mile. Taste receptors are located on their feet, or tarsi, and on the tip of the proboscis.

Butterflies and moths have hairs called tactile setae over most of their body. The setae are attached to nerve cells, which relay information about the hairs' movement. This helps the insect detect the position of one body part in relation to another.

Taxonomy

All plants and animals are named and classified using the binomial system put forth by Carl Linnaeus in 1758. Two Latin names, the first for the genus and the second for the species, are assigned to each organism. Butterflies and moths belong to the huge group, or class, called Insecta. The class is divided into smaller groups, termed orders, based on unique characteristics. The bodies of butterflies and moths are completely covered in scales. Because of this characteristic, they are placed in the order Lepidoptera—from the Ancient Greek words *lepis*, meaning "scale," and *pteron*, meaning "wing." The order is then further sorted into superfamilies, families, genera, and species.

Approximately 250,000 species of Lepidoptera have been formally named, of which only 18,000 to 20,000 are butterflies. Scientists have recently estimated that another 250,000 moths have yet to be discovered and named. If that is true, butterflies constitute less than 5 percent of the Lepidoptera species alive today. Moths are classified into 118 families while butterflies are classified into these 6: the swallowtails (Papilionidae), the whites and sulphurs (Pieridae), the brush-footed butterflies (Nymphalidae), the gossamer wings (Lycaenidae), the skippers (Hesperiidae), and the metalmarks (Riodinidae).

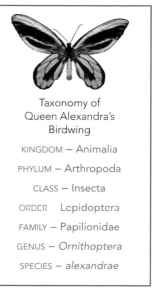

Taxonomy of
Queen Alexandra's
Birdwing

KINGDOM — Animalia

PHYLUM — Arthropoda

CLASS — Insecta

ORDER — Lepidoptera

FAMILY — Papilionidae

GENUS — *Ornithoptera*

SPECIES — *alexandrae*

The largest and most diverse family is the brush-footed, whose members appear to have only four legs because the front pair is greatly reduced in size and held close to the body. Members of eight moth families and all six butterfly families are represented in the one hundred species chosen for the paper projects.

How to Use the Field Guide

Later in this book, you will find a field guide to one hundred butterflies and moths from around the world. They are organized by their **families** and listed with their **common names** and their *Latin names*.

Butterfly or Moth?

Butterflies and moths are extremely similar, and it can be quite difficult to tell them apart. People often learn that moths are nocturnal and dull in color, while butterflies are brightly colored and fly during the day. This is a good generalization, but it is not always true. There are many diurnal moths that have beautiful iridescent colors. Looking at the antennae, the body, and the way the wings are held is the best way to distinguish a moth from a butterfly.

A butterfly (*Tithorea harmonia*)

Butterflies have straight antennae with a thickened club at the end, while moth antennae taper to a pointed tip and often look feathery, or plumose, with many filaments. Resting butterflies usually hold their wings closed together upright over the thorax and have a smooth, slender abdomen. Moths rest with their wings outstretched or folded roof-like over the thorax, have

A moth (*Antheraea pernyi*)

generally fatter bodies, and often look very furry because they are covered in long scales.

Although it is impossible to see on live, flying moths, the attachment of the hindwing to the forewing is another way to tell moths and butterflies apart. Most moths have a bristle-like structure, called a frenulum, which projects from the base of the hindwing and hooks into the forewing, holding the two wings together during flight. Butterflies do not have a frenulum. Instead, the hindwing base curves out into a humeral lobe, and the wings are not attached, allowing them to move independently.

The Life Cycle

During their life cycle, butterflies and moths pass through four distinct stages: egg, larva, pupa, and adult. These stages look nothing like one another, thus this type of cycle is called a complete metamorphosis. Many other insects, such as beetles, bees, and flies, also undergo complete metamorphosis. More primitive insects, such as dragonflies, grasshoppers, and cockroaches, undergo incomplete metamorphosis, passing through just three stages: egg, to nymph, to adult. Here, the nymph and adult stages look alike.

For Lepidoptera, life begins as a tiny egg from which a caterpillar, or larva, hatches and begins to eat. The larva is basically the growth stage. To grow, the caterpillar molts or sheds its exoskeleton. When an exoskeleton becomes too small, it splits, revealing a new one below. Depending on the species, the caterpillar will go through four or five growth periods, called instars, as it develops. Different species grow at different rates. For some, the larval stage may last only two or four weeks, while for others, it may take years. Duration depends on the species' diet and whether or not it suspends growth and hibernates as a way to get through the winter.

Eggs of the Great Southern White
(*Ascia monuste*)

The first larval meal is often the empty eggshell. The vast majority of caterpillars feed on plant material—either leaves, roots, or stems. A few bore tunnels into tree trunks and feed on the tough wood. Most species are very specific about the food they eat and only feed on one type of plant, which is known as the hostplant. Other species are polyphagous and feed on a variety of different plants. Yet others, like the clothes moths, feed on natural fibers, leaving holes in sweaters, blankets, and carpets. A few species are even carnivorous. Caterpillars of the Harvester butterfly (*Feniseca tarquinius*) feed on tiny insects called woolly aphids, and researchers in Hawaii have discovered

A Great Southern White caterpillar (*A. monuste*)

four moth species whose caterpillars dine on snails. Many species within the butterfly families Lycaenidae and Riodinidae, commonly known as gossamer wings and metalmarks, have a close relationship with ants. The caterpillar starts out life eating plant foliage, but then to complete its growth, the caterpillar fools ants into carrying it into their nest. The caterpillar produces a scent exactly the same as the ants', so when the ants find a caterpillar, they take it back to their nest and look after it as if it were one of their own larvae. There, the growing caterpillar dines on ant larvae and regurgitated food from the adult ants.

Eventually the caterpillar reaches maturity and forms a pupa. Both butterflies and moths pupate in the same way, but unlike butterflies, many moths produce a cocoon first. The moth caterpillar forms a cocoon by spinning a silken thread and weaving it back and forth to create a protective sheet around itself, sometimes incorporating plant material

A pair of Great Southern White chrysalides (*A. monuste*)

that may help with camouflage. For both butterflies and moths, the pupal shell is actually the final molt of the caterpillar. It is revealed as the exoskeleton is shed for the last time, and it hardens in the air. A butterfly pupa is usually known as a chrysalis.

Within the pupal shell, the caterpillar tissues break down, and its cell structures completely reorganize to form an adult. Metamorphosis may take place in just a few days, or it may take more than a year depending on the species and the climate. The point at which the butterfly or moth emerges (a process called eclosion) is triggered both by genetics and environmental factors. In butterflies, the pupal shell splits open and the adult climbs out, holding on to the empty shell while its wings dry. Moths wiggle out of the pupal shell, then must also push their way out of the cocoon, and finally, since many cocoons are formed on the ground, they climb to find a place to dry. The emerging insect is full size. It will not grow as an adult, but it looks a little strange with floppy, crumpled wings. This is a vulnerable time for butterflies and moths as they hang,

Great Southern Whites (*A. monuste*) mating

often for more than an hour, pumping hemolymph from the abdomen into the wings. When the wings are fully expanded and dry, the insect can fly, and the cycle begins again.

The adult stage of a moth or butterfly serves one function— reproduction. Changing from a slow moving, relatively sedentary caterpillar into a creature that can fly allows it to move around to find a mate and disperse eggs, and therefore its genes, over a large area.

Male butterflies may actively patrol areas looking for females, or they may perch on one tree and wait for them to pass. Males in the genus *Heliconius* perch next to a female pupa and mate as soon as she starts to emerge. But normally, when a male spots a female, he must persuade her to mate with him. This can involve elaborate courtship flights and the use of seductive pheromones. In moths it is usually the female that advertises her receptiveness to mate by releasing pheromones to attract males. When mating, the male uses claspers at the tip of his abdomen to hold on to the female's abdomen while he passes a spermatophore to fertilize her eggs. The pair may stay joined together for several hours. Males mate as often as possible, but the mating behavior of females varies with the species—some will mate only once, while others mate several times.

After mating, the female looks for suitable sites to lay her eggs. Depending on the species, eggs may be laid singly, stacked neatly in a short row, or laid in clumps. They vary greatly in appearance and color, from smooth spheres to ridged barrels or cones. The preferred location on the plant differs with the species; it may be the underside of a leaf, around a stem, or on a flower bud. Some grass-feeding species release their eggs as they fly close to the ground.

Feeding

In Lepidoptera, the diet and feeding methods are vastly different for caterpillars and adults. Caterpillars have strong jaws for chewing, but adults feed on liquids through their straw-like proboscis, the length of which varies with the species. Species feeding on nectar from flowers tend to have a longer, thinner proboscis than species that drink fruit juice or other liquids. The type of flower on which a species feeds may also determine proboscis length. Morgan's Sphinx moth (*Xanthopan morganii*) from Africa, which drinks from long tubular orchid blossoms, has a proboscis over 10 inches (25 centimeters) in length.

When not in use the proboscis is coiled and tucked close to the head between two structures called labial palps. When a butterfly wants to feed, muscles work to unroll the proboscis, and the liquid moves up by capillary action. Some moth species—such as Luna (*Actias luna*) and Cecropia (*Hyalophora cecropia*) moths—have no mouthparts and do not feed or drink as adults.

Lepidoptera adults have a more varied diet than most people imagine. The main diet for most species is flower nectar. Nectar consists mainly of water and 20 to 25 percent carbohydrates in the form of sugar. The concentration and composition of nectar varies from flower to flower and even by the time of day. Some species specialize in feeding at only one type of flower or prefer certain colors, while others visit many different types. Other species, like the Question Mark (*Polygonia interrogationis*) get their sugar fix from oozing, sticky tree sap, while the Harvester butterfly (*Feniseca tarquinius*) feeds exclusively on the honeydew secreted by woolly aphids.

The Owl butterflies (*Caligo* spp.) of the neotropics, and the genus *Charaxes* of Africa, mainly feed on fruit juices. Their short, thick proboscis is soft and cannot pierce the fruit skin, so they look for rotting fruit in trees or on the ground. A strong sense of smell leads them to fermented fruit, where they will drink for long periods of time, often getting quite intoxicated. Some fruit-feeding moths have a sharp-tipped proboscis that can pierce tough citrus rind. Their close relatives, the vampire moths, have a barbed proboscis and are known to pierce the skin of large mammals to drink blood.

Although sugar from nectar and fruit juice provides much-needed energy, butterflies and moths supplement their diets with other nutrients—salts, amino acids, and nitrogen—to help with successful reproduction. "Puddling" is a behavior practiced almost exclusively by males to acquire these nutrients. When mating, males pass

Puddling Spring Azure butterflies (*Celastrina* sp.)

to the female a packet called a spermatophore, which consists of sperm, nutrients, and mineral salts. The nuptial gift helps sustain the female and allows her to spend more time laying eggs rather than foraging for nutrients herself. In order to continue to mate successfully, males need to replace these nutrients. They do this by drinking from the moist ground along streams or around puddles to obtain dissolved minerals. Butterflies can be seen gathering in large numbers at a suitable puddling spot. Sometimes only one species is represented, but often the aggregation can include a mixture of several species.

Even more appealing to Lepidoptera are moist urine spots, perspiration, dung, bird droppings, and carrion—all of which contain much needed nitrogen and amino acids. Several species of moths in Southeast Asia specialize in sipping eye secretions from large mammals. They are known as "lachryphagous," meaning tear-drinking.

One group of neotropical butterflies, in the genus *Heliconius*, commonly known as the "longwings," are able to ingest amino acids and protein from pollen. The butterflies collect pollen grains on the outside of their proboscis, excrete an enzyme to dissolve the pollen, and then ingest the nutrient-rich liquid.

Survival Strategies, Camouflage, and Toxins

Moths and butterflies are vulnerable to predation at all stages in their life cycle. They make a tasty protein snack for spiders, birds, bats, rodents, and reptiles. They can fall prey to small parasitic wasps and flies who lay their own eggs either inside or on the surface of butterfly and moth eggs, caterpillars, and pupae. They can also catch diseases. To increase the chance of more eggs developing into adults, butterflies and moths have evolved in several ways in order to protect themselves.

The best option for a non-toxic species is to try not to be noticed by hiding in plain sight. Camouflage, or cryptic coloration, allows many species to blend in with their surroundings, appearing at first glance like leaves, moss, or bark. The Indian Leaf Wing (*Kallima paralekta*) has excellent camouflage; on the underside, its wings look exactly like a leaf with a tail that resembles a stem. Some species are cryptically colored on the underside of their wings—the surface seen when the wings are closed—but have

(K. paralekta)

dazzling colors on the upper surface. This makes it easier for the insect to hide, and also allows it to startle a predator if it is disturbed.

In addition to camouflage, some adults have eyespots as a means of defense. Large spots that look like eyes on the wings of butterflies and moths may help protect the insect in several ways. When resting in the dimly lit forest, the yellow eyespot on neotropical Owl butterflies (*Caligo* spp.) may resemble the eye of a large tree frog and thus makes the butterfly appear to be a bigger animal than it really is. The Polyphemus moth (*Antheraea polyphemus*) usually rests with its beige forewings partially covering its hindwings; if it feels threatened it pulls the forewings forward, revealing two startling "eyes" below. These spots may scare away predators, help the insect escape by distracting would-be attackers, or redirect a bird to peck at the false eyes instead of the vulnerable body.

Non-toxic caterpillars often hide during the day, only venturing out to eat at

The Long-tailed Skipper (*Urbanus proteus*)

night. Some species, like the Long-tailed Skipper butterfly (*Urbanus proteus*), roll the edge of a leaf over and secure it with silk, forming a tube in which to hide. Caterpillars of species like the bagworm moths (family Psychidae) construct and carry around a mobile case of silk, twigs, and other plant material for protection and camouflage. The Camouflaged Looper (*Synchlora aerata*) attaches bits of flower petals and other plant material to its body to help it blend in with its environment. The caterpillar of the Harvester butterfly (*Feniseca tarquinius*) spins a mat of silk and covers itself with the carcasses of the woolly aphids on which it has dined. Others rely on safety in numbers; they are gregarious, staying together in a group and spinning a large silken web to hide inside. And, like adults, many caterpillars have well-developed camouflage, closely resembling either the leaves on which they feed, fresh wet bird droppings, or twigs.

Caterpillars of other species take a more active defense strategy. Some are covered in irritating hairs or spines, while some project regurgitated food or emit nasty smells. Swallowtail butterfly larvae have an orange fleshy horn called an osmeterium, which protrudes from behind the head and gives off a pungent odor when the caterpillar senses danger. The Walnut Sphinx moth larva (*Amorpha juglandis*) hisses by forcing air through its spiracles.

There are many species that do not need to hide because they are distasteful or even poisonous to predators. Their caterpillars have evolved the ability to eat poisonous plants and store the toxins in their bodies, thus they are protected throughout metamorphosis into the adult stage. Toxic species usually advertise the fact that they are unpalatable with bold, bright colors as a warning to predators. These patterns, known as aposematic coloration, are often orange or red, or strongly contrasting black and white. The boldly striped black, white, and yellow Monarch caterpillar (*Danaus plexippus*) feeds on toxic milkweed plants to acquire cardiac glycosides that are retained in the body of the adult butterfly.

Some perfectly edible species have evolved an effective means to avoid being eaten called mimicry. They closely copy the colors, patterns, and behaviors of toxic species. The toxic species being copied is called the model; the palatable copycat is called the mimic. This phenomenon is called Batesian mimicry, after Henry Walter Bates, who first described the process in 1862. There is a second type of mimicry employed by butterflies and moths in which two species that are both toxic have evolved to resemble one another. This is known as Müllerian mimicry, named after Fritz Müller. The benefits of Batesian mimicry are immediately obvious for the mimic: that species gains protection by fooling predators into thinking it is unpalatable. In order for the process to work, the number of toxic models in an area must be larger than the number of mimics; predators learn to associate the bright color pattern with an unpleasant tasting experience and choose to avoid all butterflies and moths that show it.

Since predators recognize and remember that certain colors and patterns should be avoided, some groups of toxic species have evolved to look almost identical to one another. Fritz Müller reasoned that predators learn to avoid a color pattern more quickly when they are exposed to it more often. All the species benefit since fewer individuals are lost to predation. Müllerian mimicry is common in butterflies and moths throughout the neotropics. Butterflies in the genus *Heliconius* are particularly well-known for Müllerian mimicry.

The Hornet Moth (*Sesia apiformis*)

Some butterfly and moth species have evolved to mimic a different insect entirely. The perfectly harmless Hornet moth (family Sesiidae) is easily confused with the real thing. Costa Rican moths in the genus *Brenthia* actually resemble and behave like their own predators, jumping spiders.

Migration

Lepidoptera living in temperate areas often experience periods of unfavorable conditions, such as freezing temperatures, excessive heat, drought, or monsoons. Different tactics are used to overcome the harsh conditions. Some stay put and wait for conditions to change, but some leave.

Life is impossible for butterflies and moths in very cold temperatures, so many wait out the winter either by hibernating or by going into a state called diapause. A few butterflies, such as the Red Admiral (*Vanessa atalanta*) and Mourning Cloak (*Nymphalis antiopa*), hibernate as adults, taking shelter in attics, outbuildings, or under loose bark. Most species go into diapause—a delay in development during the egg, larval, or pupal stage. Some species with a large geographical distribution, like the Viceroy (*Limenitis archippus*), may undergo diapause in the northern part of their range where temperatures are cooler, but not in the warmer south. Environmental cues, like the arrival of warmer weather, usually trigger the end of diapause, and the butterfly or moth will then continue its life cycle.

The Mourning Cloak (*Nymphalis antiopa*)

Desert species may have to wait out long periods of drought when their food plants are unavailable. As adults, they can go through a period of inactivity called aestivation, while those in immature stages enter heat or drought-induced diapause, spending several years in the pupa stage waiting for rains to trigger plant growth.

Seasonal changes and shifts in environmental conditions prompt some butterflies and moths to move en masse to a new area—this is called migration. The North American Monarch (*Danaus plexippus*), a regular migrant, travels predetermined paths at predetermined times. Others are constant wanderers, striking out to colonize new areas, maybe in search of food plants. In many species, exceptionally good breeding years produce multitudes of caterpillars, leading to outbreak conditions; there are so many new individuals that adults must move to new areas, leading to spectacular dispersal flights. The clouds of insects can be so thick that they are hazardous to traffic.

Migratory species occur in all parts of the world. Examples are the Australian Bogong moth (*Agrotis infusa*), the Painted Lady butterfly (*Vanessa cardui*) in Europe and California, and the Purple Crow butterfly (*Euploea* spp.) in Taiwan. But the Monarch migration in North America is the most well-studied of all.

Monarch Migration

Monarch butterflies (*Danaus plexippus*) living east of the Rocky Mountains fly south every fall, heading to sites in Michoacán, Mexico, where they overwinter. Some individuals may travel over 2,500 miles (4,000 kilometers) from southern Canada to reach their destination. Monarchs to the west of the Rocky Mountains migrate to sheltered groves along the coast of California. Scientists believe that Monarchs were once a tropical species; over time they increased their range northward to take advantage of available hostplants, but they never evolved the ability to hibernate.

Monarchs that emerge from their chrysalis in late summer are slightly different from Monarchs that emerge earlier in the year, because they are in a state of reproductive diapause. Their reproductive organs have not

Monarchs during migration

fully developed, so they are not able to mate and lay eggs. Instead, some environmental cue—perhaps cooling night temperatures or shortening day length—tells them to fly south. The seemingly fragile butterflies navigate thousands of miles, most likely using a time-compensated sun compass and perhaps geographical features to find their way. In spring, after spending the winter roosting together in Oyamel fir trees, the Monarchs begin to fly north in search of milkweed, mating and laying eggs along the way. Their offspring continue the northward repopulation.

Because the Monarch migration is so predictable, scientists can study these butterflies to learn more about the routes taken, the time it takes to make the journey, if weather patterns affect the route, and if there are changes in these aspects from year to year. They are also able to monitor Monarch numbers to see how populations wax and wane.

Organizations such as Journey North work with students, teachers, volunteers, and researchers all over the United States, Canada, and Mexico to compile information on Monarch migration. They record when and where people report Monarchs during the flight south in the fall and on the spring flight north.

Monarch Watch based in Kansas and the Monarch Program based in California use tagging as a data collection method. Schools, nature centers, and volunteers of all sorts can become involved with the programs. In the fall, tagging events take place in many locations across southern Canada and the United States. Local Monarchs are caught and a tiny sticker, or tag, with a number code is attached to the hindwing. The number is recorded along with when and where the butterfly is released and all the information is sent to the corresponding organization. When anyone recovers a Monarch with a tag, they can send data to the appropriate organization, thus helping compile information on that individual monarch and migration patterns in general.

Conservation

Butterflies and moths are very sensitive to changes in their environment and are often the first organisms to disappear from an imbalanced ecosystem. They are therefore good indicators of environmental health. Most species are so dependant on their caterpillar hostplant for survival that any damage to the habitat where those plants grow reduces the population size that can be supported. A species in trouble is classified by the degree of concern for its long-term survival; the categories range from vulnerable to threatened to endangered. A species that has completely disappeared is considered extinct. When a species disappears from an area where it was formally abundant but is still found in other parts of its range, it is considered locally extinct, or extirpated.

By far the biggest threat to Lepidoptera populations is human interference in the environment. Deforestation, draining wetlands, and plowing grasslands for agriculture and urban development destroys essential habitats. Pollution also has disastrous consequences, as do activities like spraying pesticides to control other insects and introducing a foreign species into an ecosystem.

Fortunately, butterfly watching has become almost as popular a hobby as bird watching. Butterfly groups, such as the North American Butterfly Association (NABA) and the Lepidopterists' Society, offer meetings, field trips, and e-mail alerts for the latest sightings. Major tour companies conduct trips where ecotourism and butterfly watching are the main focus. This has lead to people becoming more aware of the threats to butterfly and moth species, with a corresponding increase in conservation efforts.

Numerous international and national organizations address conservation needs, and laws have been passed affording legal protection to endangered species. The International Union for Conservation of Nature (IUCN) evaluates the conservation status of all plants and animals globally and maintains a catalogue of all vulnerable, threatened, and endangered species. This data is known as the IUCN Red List of Threatened Species. Many governments use this information to develop their own conservation priorities. In 1975, the Convention on International Trade in Endangered Species of Wild Fauna and Flora (CITES) solidified agreements between countries to control the trade of listed species. The Xerces Society, named after the now extinct Xerces Blue butterfly

The Xerces Blue *(Glaucopsyche xerces)*

(*Glaucopsyche xerces*), develops conservation programs to protect invertebrates and their habitats worldwide.

These large organizations work with smaller organizations at a local level to implement conservation initiatives. Habitat protection is critically important in maintaining Lepidoptera populations. Habitat restoration, the act of removing introduced plant species and encouraging growth of native plants, is often a priority. Sometimes more than one approach is needed, such as habitat management along with a captive breeding program. In a captive breeding program, caterpillars are raised in a laboratory where they are protected from natural predators; a much larger percentage grows to be adults. The adults are reintroduced into the wild and the population is carefully monitored. Captive breeding programs have proved successful in the conservation of endangered butterflies such as the Miami Blue (*Hemiargus thomasi bethunebakeri*).

Butterfly Species

Papilionidae

Bhutan Glory
Bhutanitis lidderdalei

Range: Bhutan, northeastern India, northern Myanmar, Thailand, and southern China

The Bhutan Glory has a slow, unpredictable, fluttery flight and may be unpalatable to predators since the larvae feed on poisonous plants in the genus *Aristolochia*. These butterflies are very popular with collectors.

Five-striped Kite Swallowtail
Protesilaus protesilaus

Range: Mexico, south to Paraguay

All of the Kite Swallowtails have a strong, fast flight. They prefer to fly high at treetop level, but males come to the ground to puddle.

Tailed Jay
Graphium agamemnon

Range: India and Bangladesh, through Southeast Asia to New Guinea and northern Australia

> The Tailed Jay can complete its life cycle in a little over one month, and usually there are seven to eight broods per year. The female has longer tails than the male.

Purple Spotted Swallowtail
Graphium weiskei

Range: Papua New Guinea

> Although the Purple Spotted Swallowtail has a restricted range, it is quite common. It prefers mountainous regions, usually flying at altitudes of over 4,000 feet (1,219 meters).

Green Dragontail
Lamproptera meges

Range: India and Southeast Asia

The Green Dragontail has transparent areas on the forewings, which are devoid of scales. In flight, the wings flutter rapidly and the butterfly hovers over flowers to feed like a hummingbird.

Queen Alexandra's Birdwing
Ornithoptera alexandrae

Range: Southeastern Papua New Guinea

The Queen Alexandra's Birdwing is the largest butterfly in the world, with a wingspan of up to 11 inches (28 cm). The species is sexually dimorphic; the brightly-colored, iridescent males (shown here) are smaller than the dull-colored females. It is listed by the IUCN as an endangered species, which is mainly due to destruction of its preferred habitat—old-growth rainforest. It is highly prized by collectors, and one specimen can fetch thousands of dollars.

African Giant Swallowtail
Papilio antimachus

Range: Central and West Africa, from
Uganda to Sierra Leone and south
to Angola

> This swallowtail is the largest butterfly
> on the African continent. The bright
> orange coloration serves as a warning
> to predators that this species is highly
> toxic, containing large quantities of
> cardenolide poisons acquired as a
> caterpillar from its hostplant.

Mocker Swallowtail
Papilio dardanus

Range: Wet forests of Africa and
Madagascar

> The female Mocker Swallowtail has no
> hindwing tails. It shows many different
> color forms, mimicking several other
> butterfly species throughout its range.
> This butterfly is also known as the
> Flying Handkerchief.

Tiger Swallowtail
Heraclides glaucus

Range: North America, from Canada to the Gulf of Mexico

The early instar larvae resemble bird droppings for protection. This is one of the few swallowtails that accepts many different hostplants. The caterpillars feed on tulip trees, wild cherries, and cottonwoods. The female occurs in two color forms: a yellow form similar to the male, and a dark form in the southern part of the species' range that is most likely a mimic of the toxic Pipevine Swallowtail (*Battus philenor*).

Homerus Swallowtail
Heraclides homerus

Range: Jamaica

With a wingspan of 6 inches (15 centimeters), the Homerus Swallowtail is the largest butterfly in the western hemisphere. It has been listed as an endangered species since 1987.

Great Mormon
Papilio memnon

Range: Northeastern India, through Myanmar, across southern China and Southeast Asia to Indonesia and Japan

Female Great Mormon butterflies are polymorphic and mimic several different unpalatable species, such as the Common Rose (*Pachliopta aristolochiae*), an unrelated Swallowtail.

Emerald Swallowtail
Papilio palinurus

Range: Southeast Asia

This species is also known as the Banded Peacock. The iridescent green on the upper surface of the wings is due to the structural surface of the scales mixing reflected blue and yellow light.

Green-celled Cattleheart
Parides childrenae

Range: Southern Mexico to Ecuador

Larvae of the Green-celled Cattleheart acquire toxins by feeding on *Aristolochia* vines. The male and female are sexually dimorphic—the male (shown here) has large green patches on the forewing, but these are absent in the female.

Apollo
Parnassius apollo

Range: Mountainous areas of Europe and Central Asia

The preferred habitat of the Apollo is high altitude rocky meadows, up to 6,500 feet (2,000 meters) above sea level. It overwinters as an egg. The larvae feed on stonecrop plants in the genus *Sedum*. This species has hundreds of named subspecies within its range, some confined to a single valley.

Rajah Brooke's Birdwing
Trogonoptera brookiana

Range: Sumatra, Borneo, and the Malaysian peninsula

This species was first described by Alfred Russel Wallace in 1855, and named after Sir James Brooke, Rajah of Sarawak. The larvae feed on *Aristolochia* vines. Adults can be seen feeding on nectar and fruit juices, and males congregate together to puddle on stream banks.

Spanish Festoon
Zerynthia rumina

Range: Spain, Portugal, southeastern France, and North Africa

The Spanish Festoon, one of the smallest members of the Swallowtail family, has no tails. It overwinters in the pupal stage.

Pieridae

White Angled Sulphur
Anteos clorinde

Range: Southern United States, West Indies, and Mexico south to Paraguay

The White Angled Sulphur, sometimes known as the Clorinde, is a very fast flier. The pale green, veined underwings allow it to blend in with its surroundings.

Purple Tip
Colotis ione

Range: Dry areas of Africa except real desert and subdesert

The wing tips of Purple Tip males (shown here) are a stunning violet, but the color varies greatly in females.

Tiger Mimic White
Dismorphia amphiona

Range: Mexico, Central and South America

Studying Amazonian members of the
genus *Dismorphia* in the mid-1800s
led Henry Walter Bates to develop his
theory of mimicry.

Brimstone
Gonepteryx rhamni

Range: Europe, Asia, and North Africa

In Britain, the Brimstone overwinters as
an adult and is often the first species to
be seen in the spring. It has often been
claimed that this species gave us the
name *butterfly*, a corruption of the word
for butter-colored fly.

Great Orange Tip
Hebomoia glaucippe

Range: India to China and Japan,
Australasia

This species is a fast, powerful flier.
Males often congregate on moist stream
banks for puddling. When the butterfly
is at rest, it is well camouflaged because
the undersides of the wings look like a
dead leaf.

California Dogface
Zerene eurydice

Range: California and occasionally western
Arizona in the United States

The unusual forewing markings,
which resemble a dog's face, occur only
on males. This species has been the
California state insect since 1972.

Nymphalidae

Celerio Sister
Adelpha serpa

Range: Mexico south to Brazil and Paraguay

There are eighty-five species in the neotropical genus *Adelpha*, most with very similar wing patterns. Adults feed on both nectar and rotting fruit.

Mountain Pride
Aeropetes tulbaghia

Range: South Africa and Zimbabwe

The Mountain Pride prefers to feed at red and orange flowers. It is the only known pollinator of the red disa orchid.

Small Tortoiseshell
Aglais urticae

Range: Europe, and across temperate Asia to Japan

The Small Tortoiseshell hibernates as an adult, often taking shelter in attics and undisturbed buildings. The larvae feed on stinging nettles.

Claudina
Agrias claudina

Range: Ecuador, Peru, and Brazil

Members of the genus *Agrias* are highly prized by collectors due to their stunning coloration and intricately patterned undersides.

Gulf Fritillary
Agraulis vanillae

Range: Argentina, north to Caribbean and southern United States; occasionally migrates farther north

The Gulf Fritillary is a member of the subfamily Heliconiinae, commonly known as "passion flower butterflies," since the caterpillars of most species feed on *Passiflora*. Like most fritillaries, this butterfly has spectacular silver spots on the underside of its wings.

White Peacock
Anartia jatrophae

Range: Southern United States and Central America south to Argentina

The dry season form of the White Peacock is larger and paler than the wet season form (shown here). This species prefers moist habitats along streams or around ponds.

Sapphira Blue
Asterope sapphira

Range: Lower Amazon of Brazil

Members of the genus *Asterope* prefer dense, undisturbed forest habitat. Adults are attracted to dung and rotting fruit.

Blue Duke
Bassarona durga

Range: Northeastern India

The Blue Duke is an endangered species found only in the hilly state of Nagaland, India.

Spotted Shoemaker
Catonephele numilia

Range: Mexico, south to Argentina

Spotted Shoemakers are sexually dimorphic. Six orange spots on velvet black wings easily distinguish the male (shown here) from the female, who has a creamy white stripe across the forewing.

Owl Butterfly
Caligo atreus

Range: Mexico to Peru

Members of the genus *Caligo* are easily recognized by the large eyespots on the underside of the hindwings, giving them their common name, Owl butterflies. This species is crepuscular, meaning that it usually flies at dawn and dusk.

Common Wood Nymph
Cercyonis pegala

Range: Southern Canada to northern Mexico

The Common Wood Nymph overwinters as a newly hatched caterpillar. Adults feed on both fruit juice and nectar.

Malay Lacewing
Cethosia hypsea

Range: Myanmar, through the Malaysian Peninsula to Sumatra

The Malay Lacewing is distasteful to predators. The intricate pattern on the underside of the wings probably gave rise to its common name.

Blue Spotted Charaxes
Charaxes cithaeron

Range: Southern Africa

Species in the genus *Charaxes* have strong, powerful flight. Adults seek out rotting, fermenting fruit and can become quite intoxicated while feeding.

Crimson Patch
Chlosyne janais

Range: Southern Texas, through Central America to Colombia

The Crimson Patch prefers wooded and scrub habitats close to streams. Females lay eggs in large batches on the underside of leaves.

Paradise Phantom
Cithaerias phantoma

Range: Colombia, Ecuador, Peru, and Brazil

Members of the genus *Cithaerias* are characterized by wings that are entirely transparent, except for a small patch of color and an eyespot on the hindwing. The preferred habitat is dense rainforest, where the adults fly low to the ground in the dark forest understory.

Tiger Leafwing
Consul fabius

Range: Mexico, south to Brazil

The Tiger Leafwing mimics several members of the genus *Heliconius*, as well as some butterflies in the subfamily Ithomiinae. The underside of the wings has cryptic coloration, and when resting, the butterfly resembles a dead leaf.

Hobart's Red Glider
Cymothoe hobarti

Range: Central Africa, Cameroon to western Kenya

The preferred habitat of Hobart's Red Glider is dense rainforest. Females tend to be more variable in coloration than males (shown here).

Common Map
Cyrestis thyodamas

Range: India, east through Myanmar and Thailand to southern China and Japan

Species in the genus *Cyrestis* are noted for the attractive lined patterns on the wings, giving rise to the name map butterflies. Common Map larvae feed on the leaves of fig trees (genus *Ficus*).

Plain Tiger
Danaus chrysippus

Range: Widespread throughout Asia, the Middle East, and Africa; also found in Australia

The Plain Tiger is closely related to the Monarch butterfly (*Danaus plexippus*). The adults, larvae, and chrysalides look very similar. Caterpillars of both species feed on milkweed and are distasteful to predators.

Monarch
Danaus plexippus

Range: North, Central, and South America; Australia; the Philippines; and Papua New Guinea; a rare migrant into Western Europe

The larvae feed on milkweed plants, acquiring toxic cardiac glycosides, which make the caterpillars and adults distasteful to predators. The Monarch is a well-known migrant in North America. Some travel from Canada to overwintering grounds in Mexico.

Forest Queen
Euxanthe wakefieldi

Range: Tropical East Africa, from Kenya south to South Africa

The Forest Queen prefers coastal forest habitats, where males (shown here) often patrol territories in clearings and along forest edges. Females lack the male's turquoise coloration, appearing more black and white. This species is characterized by rounded forewings.

Baltimore Checkerspot
Euphydryas phaeton

Range: North America, Nova Scotia west to Manitoba, and south through the eastern United States to Georgia

Baltimore Checkerspot larvae feed together in a communal web, but in the fourth instar, they move off the hostplant to hibernate among leaves on the ground. They continue growing in the spring.

Red Cracker
Hamadryas amphinome

Range: Mexico to the Amazon Basin, Peru, and Bolivia

Species in the genus *Hamadryas* get their common name, cracker butterflies, from the clicking noise produced by the male's forewings. Adults feed on rotting fruit.

Cydno Longwing
Heliconius cydno

Range: Southern Mexico, through Central America south to Venezuela, Colombia, and Ecuador

Like other members of the genus *Heliconius*, larvae of the Cydno Longwing feed on passion vine (*Passiflora*) and are distasteful to predators. Adults not only feed on nectar but also collect pollen on their proboscis, which they ingest in liquid form by excreting an enzyme to dissolve the pollen.

Small Postman
Heliconius erato

Range: Mexico to the Amazon Basin

The Small Postman occurs in many color forms throughout its range. At each location, it occurs as a perfect Müllerian mimic of a different *Heliconius* species, *H. melpomene*. Adults roost together in small groups, often returning to precisely the same twig or branch night after night.

Stinky Leaf Wing
Historis odius

Range: Southern United States, through Central America and northern South America

The Stinky Leaf Wing probably gets its common name from the fact that adults are strongly attracted to rotting fruit and dung to feed. This species has a fast, powerful flight.

Gladiator
Hypolimnas dexithea

Range: Madagascar

The Gladiator is one of the larger members of the genus *Hypolimnas*.

Red Spot Diadem
Hypolimnas usambara

Range: Coastal Kenya and eastern Tanzania

The Red Spot Diadem prefers dense forest habitat, where the larvae feed on plants in the nettle family (Urticaceae).

Paper Kite
Idea leuconoe

Range: Thailand to Malaysia and the Philippines, Taiwan, and Borneo

The Paper Kite is also known as the Large Tree Nymph and the Rice Paper butterfly. It exhibits a slow, gliding flight. The chrysalis is a brilliant, shiny gold with black markings.

Peacock
Inachis io

Range: Europe, east across temperate Asia to Japan

The bold eyespots on the upper surface of the Peacock's wings are a sharp contrast to the dull brown undersides. The larvae feed on nettles and hops. This species hibernates as an adult in attics, outbuildings, and under loose bark.

Common Buckeye
Junonia coenia

Range: Southern Canada to Mexico, Bermuda, and Cuba

The Common Buckeye is a year-round resident in the southern United States but also disperses north into the northern states and southern Canada during the spring and summer. It is easily recognized by the distinctive eyespots on its wings. Larvae feed on plants in the snapdragon and plantain families.

Yellow Pansy
Junonia hierta

Range: Africa, the Arabian Peninsula, India, and Sri Lanka to Myanmar, the Malaysian Peninsula, and southern and western China

Yellow Pansy adults feed on nectar, but they can also be seen feeding on carrion and dung. Larvae feed on plants in the genus *Acanthus*.

Gaudy Commodore
Precis octavia

Range: Throughout Africa south of the Sahara

The Gaudy Commodore has two different color forms. The wet season form is a pinkish orange, while the dry season form (shown here) is purple.

Indian Leaf Wing
Kallima paralekta

Range: India and Pakistan to southern and central China, Taiwan, and Japan

This species is also known as the Orange Oak Leaf and Dead Leaf butterfly. When the wings are closed, this butterfly has almost perfect camouflage. The distinct vein on the brown underside of the wings, coupled with their shape and the hindwing tail resembling a stem, give this butterfly the appearance of a dead leaf.

Archduke
Lexias pardalis

Range: Southeast Asia

The Archduke is sexually dimorphic; the male has a wide lilac rim on the black hindwings, whereas the female (shown here) has yellow dots across the forewings and hindwings.

Ruddy Daggerwing
Marpesia petreus

Range: Southern United States, Central and South America

Larvae of the Ruddy Daggerwing feed on various species of fig and cashew. Adult males can be seen puddling, where they take up dissolved salts. The preferred habitats are tropical and subtropical forests.

Polymnia Tigerwing
Mechanitis polymnia

Range: Mexico, south to Ecuador and Brazil

Members of the genus *Mechanitis* are toxic models for *Dismorphia* species, which are palatable.

Blue Morpho
Morpho cypris

Range: Colombia, Ecuador, Peru, and Brazil

The brilliant, iridescent blue coloration of butterflies in this genus results from the way the wing scales reflect light. Females of *M. cypris* have no blue coloration at all, but are instead yellow, orange, and brown.

Blue Wave
Myscelia cyaniris

Range: Mexico to south Peru

This species is also known as the
Banded Purple Wing, Whitened
Bluewing, and Royal Blue. The blue
bands are less iridescent on the female.
Adult Blue Waves feed on rotting fruit.

Mourning Cloak
Nymphalis antiopa

Range: Europe, temperate Asia, North
America, and Mexico

This butterfly is known as the
Mourning Cloak in North America
and the Camberwell Beauty in Europe.
It overwinters as an adult, and in North
America it is often the first species seen
in early spring.

Clipper
Parthenos sylvia

Range: India and Sri Lanka, through the Malaysian peninsula to the Philippines and Papua New Guinea

The Clipper has characteristic white spots on the forewing, but hindwing coloration varies from blue to greenish to orange and brown across its range. Consequently, it is known in some areas as the Blue Clipper and in others as the Brown Clipper.

Question Mark
Polygonia interrogationis

Range: Southern Canada, south through the eastern United States to Florida and Mexico

This species gets its common name from the tiny silver question mark shape on the hindwing underside. The butterfly occurs in two forms: the summer form is darker, whereas the winter form (shown here) is more orange with a violet hindwing margin.

Forest Mother-of-pearl
Salamis parhassus

Range: Throughout tropical Africa, except the western Cape Province

This species and others in the genus derive their common name from the mother-of-pearl-like luster of their wings. Males of *S. parhassus* perch at vantage points in their preferred forest habitat and will fly out to investigate anything white, such as someone waving a white handkerchief.

Malachite
Siproeta stelenes

Range: Brazil north through Central America into southern Texas, the West Indies, and southern Florida

Adult Malachite butterflies feed on rotting fruit, bird droppings, dung, and carrion, but will also visit flowers for nectar. The Malachite's chrysalis is shiny pale green, adorned with golden spikes.

Silky Owl
Taenaris phorcas

Range: Solomon Islands

The Silky Owl prefers a dense forest habitat, where it feeds on rotting fruit.

Kamehameha
Vanessa tameamea

Range: Hawaii

The Kamehameha is one of only two butterfly species endemic to Hawaii. Adults feed on the sap of Koa trees, while larvae feed on native nettle species.

The Lurcher
Yoma sabina

Range: Northern Australia, north into Southeast Asia

Females (shown here) have a white mark in the black tips of the forewings and black dots within the yellow band, while males have a yellow forewing mark and lack the black dots.

Lycaenidae
Hewitson's Blue Hairstreak
Evenus coronata

Range: Southern Mexico through Central America to Colombia, Ecuador, and Peru

Also known as the Crowned Hairstreak, this species was described by Hewitson in 1865. Red patches on the female's hindwings differentiate her from the male (shown here).

Harvester

Feniseca tarquinius

Range: Eastern United States

Harvester butterflies have a close relationship not with plants, but with another insect. Females lay eggs in woolly aphid colonies and the caterpillars feed on the aphids. Adult Harvesters do not visit flowers for nectar but sip the honeydew produced by woolly aphids.

Xerces Blue

Glaucopsyche xerces

Range: Extinct

The Xerces Blue was last seen in 1941. This is the first North American butterfly known to have become extinct due to human disturbance; its preferred sand dune habitat gradually shrank as a result of urban development. The Xerces Society, established in 1971 to help protect threatened and endangered invertebrates, takes its name from this butterfly.

Scarce Copper
Lycaena virgaureae

Range: Europe, east across Asia to Siberia and Mongolia

Males (shown here) of this species display the bright coppery coloration that gives the family Lycaenidae one of their common names. Females are more subdued in color, being speckled with brown. This species overwinters as an egg.

Hesperiidae
Indian Awlking
Choaspes benjaminii

Range: India, Sri Lanka, northern Myanmar, Malaysia, and Japan

The Indian Awlking lives in dense jungle habitat.

Regent Skipper
Euschemon rafflesia

Range: Queensland, Australia

This species is unique among butterflies; its wings are joined together by a frenulum, a bristle-like structure on the hindwing that fits into a hook on the forewing. The frenulum is found in all male moths but not in butterflies, except for the male Regent Skipper.

Long-tailed Skipper
Urbanus proteus

Range: Southern United States, south through Central and South America to Argentina, West Indies

The Long-tailed Skipper is also known as the Bean Leafroller, because the larvae fold over a leaf of their hostplant to form a shelter. This species is a pest on legume crops such as peas, lima beans, and soybeans.

Riodinidae

Formosissima Swordtail
Ancyluris formosissima

Range: Ecuador and Peru

> Adults in this genus prefer to feed at white and yellow flowers.

Giant Metalmark
Behemothia godmanii

Range: Central Mexico to Costa Rica

> The Giant Metalmark is one of the largest members in the family Riodinidae.

Great Eurybia
Eurybia patrona

Range: Honduras to Panama

Members of the genus *Eurybia* have unusually long proboscises, typically one and a half times the length of the body.

Dyson's Swordtail
Rhetus dysonii

Range: Costa Rica to Peru and Brazil

Members of this genus are fast flying. During long periods of dry weather, the males feed on fresh bird droppings.

Moth Species

Uraniidae
Madagascan Sunset Moth
Chrysiridia rhipheus

Range: Madagascar

The Madagascan Sunset moth flies during the day. The caterpillars feed on plants in the genus *Omphalea* (family Euphorbiaceae), making the larvae and adults toxic to predators. The moth's brilliant, iridescent colors are due to light reflecting from the wing scales.

Brahmaeidae
Owl Moth
Brahmaea wallichii

Range: Northern India, through Myanmar to Nepal, China, and Japan

Male Owl moths are smaller than females. The larvae feed on privet and lilac (family Oleaceae).

Saturniidae
Atlas Moth
Attacus atlas

Range: India, across tropical Southeast Asia to Indonesia

The Atlas moth has the largest wing surface area of any moth in the world. Females (shown here) are much larger and heavier than males, though males have larger feathery antennae. Like all species in the family Saturniidae, the Atlas moth has no proboscis and does not feed as an adult.

Io Moth
Automeris io

Range: Southern Canada and the United States, east of the Rocky Mountains, south through Mexico to Costa Rica

Larvae of the Io moth are polyphagous, feeding on a wide variety of trees. This species is sexually dimorphic—the male is smaller with yellow forewings, while the female (shown here) is reddish brown.

Spanish Moon Moth
Graellsia isabellae

Range: Spain and France

Spanish Moon moth larvae feed on pine needles. The moth overwinters in its cocoon.

Speckled Emperor
Gynanisa maja

Range: Southern Africa, north to Angola and Zambia

Larvae of the Speckled Emperor moth are one of several edible species traditionally harvested for centuries by the Bisa people of northern Zambia. Caterpillars provide local families additional protein in their diet and an extra source of income through trade.

Golden Emperor
Loepa katinka

Range: Northern India, east throughout Southeast Asia

Male Golden Emperor moths are slightly smaller than females (shown here) and are distinguished by having more pointed forewings.

Sphingidae
Death's Head Hawkmoth
Acherontia atropos

Range: Southern Europe and Africa

Adult Death's Head Hawkmoths enter beehives to feed on honey. When it feels threatened, the moth squeaks by forcing air out of its proboscis. The common name comes from the skull-like pattern on the moth's thorax. This species was made famous in the book and movie *Silence of the Lambs*.

Verdant Sphinx
Euchloron megaera

Range: Africa, south of the Sahara desert

Larvae of the Verdant Sphinx feed on
grape vines and Virginia creeper.

One-eyed Sphinx
Smerinthus cerisyi

Range: North America

Larvae of the One-eyed Sphinx feed on
willow and poplar trees.

Morgan's Sphinx
Xanthopan morganii

Range: Tropical Africa and Madagascar

In 1862, Charles Darwin predicted the existence of a moth with a proboscis that extended 10–11 inches (25.4–28 cm) to pollinate the unusually long, trumpet-shaped nectary of the Madagascan orchid *Angraecum sesquipedale*. The moth was discovered in 1903.

Arctiidae

Great Tiger Moth
Arctia caja

Range: Europe, across temperate Asia to Japan; occasionally in Canada and the northern United States

This toxic species is also known as the Garden Tiger. The hindwings vary from deep orange to yellow.

Giant Leopard Moth
Hypercompe scribonia

Range: Southeastern Canada, through the eastern United States to Mexico

The bristly larvae of the Giant Leopard moth feed on a wide variety of hostplants including cherry, maple, and dandelion.

Four-spotted Tiger
Hyperthaema sanguineata

Range: Colombia, Ecuador, Peru, and Bolivia

The blood-red coloration of the Four-spotted Tiger moth warns would-be predators that it is toxic.

Sesiidae

Hornet Moth
Sesia apiformis

Range: Europe into eastern Asia; and eastern North America

This diurnal moth bears an incredible resemblance to a hornet; it even mimics the wasp's jerky flight pattern. Larvae feed by boring into the wood of willows and poplars.

Noctuidae

Aholibah Underwing
Catocala aholibah

Range: Western North America

All members of the *Catocala* genus rest with their cryptic forewings covering the hindwings. When disturbed, the moth startles would-be attackers by flashing the bright underwings.

African Peach Moth
Egybolis vaillantina

Range: Africa, south of the Sahara desert

The brilliantly-colored African Peach moth is diurnal. Larvae feed on peach and soapberry.

Owlet Moth
Peridrome orbicularis

Range: Eastern Himalaya, through Myanmar and Thailand to the Philippines and Borneo

Females of this species are slightly larger than males. Larvae feed on plants in the dogbane family.

White Witch
Thysania agrippina

Range: South America, north to Mexico

The White Witch is also known as the Ghost moth or Great Owlet. It is one of the largest moth species, with a wingspan of up to 12 inches (30.5 cm).

Megalopygidae
Cotton Candy Flannel Moth
Trosia punctigera

Range: Panama, Colombia, Guyana, Surinam, and Brazil

The Flannel moth family occurs mainly in the neotropics. Soft outer hairs on the larvae mask long stinging spines that can cause a rash and inflammation if handled.

Paper Butterfly Projects

Butterfly Flyers

This is an easy way to turn a paper butterfly into a bona fide butterfly flyer. To make this project you will need scissors and clear tape. Some measurements may need to be slightly adjusted depending on the moth or butterfly you pick.

1. Punch out the butterfly or moth.
2. From the leftover paper, cut two strips that are each about 1" wide and the length of the paper.
3. Fold the Flyer in half lengthwise along the center of the body so the full-color wings come up and meet each other.
4. Holding the Flyer by the body, fold down the wings approximately ¾" from the body. Make the folds even, so the wings are folded down as symmetrically as possible.
5. Now, take one of the strips you cut in step two, and starting from one end and working towards the other, fold the strip of paper over on itself to create ½" × 1" bundles. Tape the bundle so it does not unfold. Repeat with the second strip.
6. Tape one bundle to the front underside of each of the butterfly wings as shown in the photograph. Cut off any excess of the bundle and tape that is hanging past the edge of the wing.
7. Hold the body of the Flyer like a paper airplane and throw it forward levelly, like a dart.

Butterfly Flying Tips

- If the butterfly dives down, gently bend the front wing tips up to give the butterfly more lift.
- To make a stunt butterfly flyer, bend the back wing tips up or down and see what happens!
- These butterflies and moths make the best Flyers:

  Bhutan Glory, Purple Spotted Swallowtail, Mocker Swallowtail, Tiger Swallowtail, Emerald Swallowtail, Green-celled Cattlehart, Apollo, White Angled Sulphur, Gladiator, Red Spot Diadem, Peacock, Gaudy Commodore, Indian Leaf Wing, Archduke, Ruddy Daggerwing, Mourning Cloak, Forest Mother-of-pearl, Silky Owl, Formosissima Swordtail, Giant Metalmark, Dyson's Swordtail, Madagascan Sunset moth, Owl moth, Speckled Emperor, and White Witch

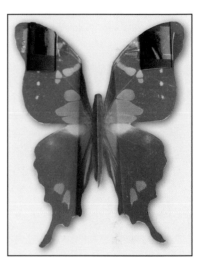

Butterfly Gliders

Some butterflies migrate from one part of the world to another. This glider will ensure that these paper butterflies have a safe trip. To make this project, pick a butterfly or moth, find a piece of paper, scissors, and clear tape, as well as a length of dental floss, fishing wire, or thread.

1. Punch out a butterfly or moth.
2. From the leftover paper, cut a strip that is 2" wide and the length of the butterfly or moth's body.
3. Roll the strip of paper into a thin tube. Tape it to prevent it from unrolling.
4. Fold the butterfly or moth in half lengthwise along the center of the body so the blue colored wings come up and meet each other.
5. Tape the tube to the blue side of the butterfly's body along the fold.
6. Run the thread through the tube, and watch the butterfly fly on its path overhead. If the thread moves up and down, the butterfly flaps its wings!

Butterfly Glider Tip

- String up multiple butterflies across your ceiling. Several butterflies can glide on a single string, or they can crisscross around the room.
- You can replace the paper tube with a colorful drinking straw.

Pinning Butterflies

Pinning butterflies and moths is the traditional way to display these beautiful creatures. You can pin them to a foam mounting board, your walls, or a cork board. You will need straight pins or thumbtacks.

1. Punch out a butterfly or moth. If you like, you can cut out the antennae and glue them on to the head.
2. Fold the wings up along the body.
3. Pin down the body and the tips of the wings. When pinning down the wing tips, do not lay them flat; instead, push them slightly toward the body so they bow up just a bit, giving the specimen depth.

Tips:
- You can mount your butterflies one at a time or in groups.
- If you are mounting several butterflies to one surface, you can make neat rows in the traditional way, or you can stagger and layer them in any pattern you like.

Alternatives:
- Instead of pinning, you can mount these butterflies and moths by gluing down the body and wings to a sheet of construction paper. You can then frame and/or hang the paper.
- For another beautiful project, you can punch out the butterflies and decoupage them to any surface.

Butterfly Mobile

It is fun to display beautiful butterflies. Try this mobile for a more advanced project. To build this design, use a ruler, a pencil, letter paper, scissors, tape, and a needle and thread.

1. Holding a piece of letter paper with the short edge at top, fold it in half from left to right three times creating eight identical rectangular panels. Repeat this process with a second piece of paper. These will be used to create the long tubes.

2. Unfold each piece of paper and cut them in half using the middle fold as a guide. There should be four pieces of paper each folded into four panels.

3. Fold one of these pieces of paper in half lengthwise to find the midpoint. Cut it in half to create two pieces of paper, each 5-½" in length. Set these aside; they will be used later to create the short tubes.

4. Using a piece of long tube paper, follow the diagram for Tubes #1 and #2. String 8" of thread through starred points A and B. *A should be centered exactly on the right-most crease. *B should be centered on the second panel from the left. String 5" of thread through starred points C and D. *C and *D should be centered on the second panel from the left, exactly 2-¾" from the ends. (See Diagram 1.)

5. Secure all of the threads with pieces of tape. One side of the paper should have short pieces of thread secured by tape, and the other side should have long threads hanging from it. This is Tube #1.

6. Repeat step 4 with a second piece of long tube paper, this time using 5" lengths of string, to create Tube #2. There is one slight variation from the process described in step 4: thread Tube #1 *B with the string from Tube #2 *A, thereby attaching the two tubes.

Tubes #1 & #2

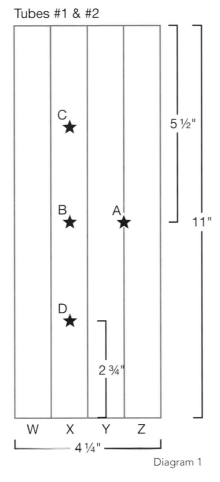

C ★

B ★　A ★

D ★

5 ½"

11"

2 ¾"

W　X　Y　Z

└── 4 ¼" ──┘

Diagram 1

7. Repeat Step 5.

8. Now it's time to fold these pieces into tubes. Fold Tube #1 and Tube #2 around so that the taped ends of the thread are left inside and the long ends outside. Tape the inside of Panel Z to the outside of Panel W. The result is two triangular tubes connected to each other by one thread. (See Diagram 2.)

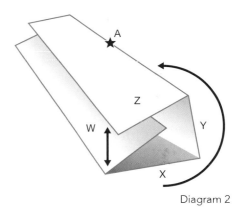

A ★

Z

W　Y

X

Diagram 2

9. Use the remaining pieces of unfolded paper to create Tubes #3 and #4.

10. Following the diagram, thread a 10" piece of string through * on Tubes #3 and #4. (See Diagram 3.)

11. To fold #3 and #4 into short tubes, follow the instructions from Step 8.

12. Tape the thread coming from * on Tubes #3 and #4 inside the ends of Tube #1. Tubes #3 and #4 now hang about 2" below Tube #2. Tape 3" pieces of string inside each end of Tubes #3 and #4.

13. The structure for the mobile is now complete. It's time to punch out butterflies and attach them to the threads on the mobile. Using the threads attached to the mobile, poke through the tops of the butterflies with a needle. Use small pieces of tape on the bottoms to make them neatly secure.

Tubes #3 & #4

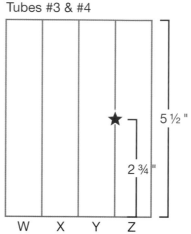

Diagram 3

Hang your mobile anywhere you want to enjoy elegant butterflies.

Variation:
Instead of making paper tubes, you can use sticks and twigs to make the structure for your mobile.

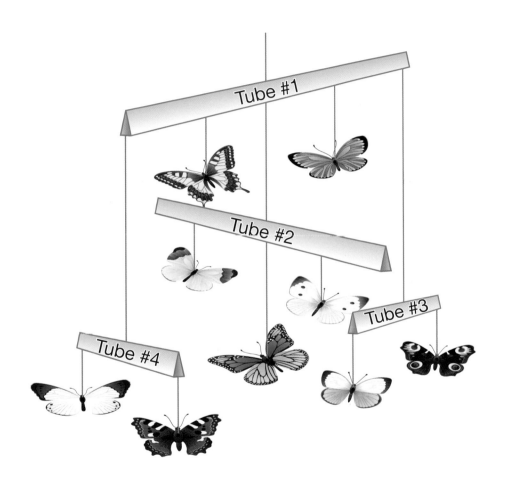

Tube #1

Tube #2

Tube #3

Tube #4

References

Carter, D. 1992. *Eyewitness Handbook to Butterflies and Moths.* London: DK Publishing, Inc.

Daniels, J.C. & Sanchez, S.J. 2006. "Blues' Revival: Can a Change in Diet—and a Little Laboratory Assistance—Help a Florida Butterfly Escape Extinction." *Natural History.* 26–28 October.

Davies, H. & Butler, C.A. 2008. *Do Butterflies Bite? Fascinating Answers to Questions about Butterflies and Moths.* New Jersey: Rutgers University Press

DeVries, P.J. 1987. *The Butterflies of Costa Rica and Their Natural History, Vol I: Papilionidae, Pieridae, Nymphalidae.* New Jersey: Princeton University Press

DeVries, P.J. 1997. *The Butterflies of Costa Rica and Their Natural History, Vol II: Riodinidae.* New Jersey: Princeton University Press

Frome, A. 2005. "Edible Insects." *Zoogoer.* July/August

Hofmann, H. and Marktanner, T. 2001. *Collins Nature Guide to Butterflies and Moths of Britain and Europe.* London: HarperCollins

Hoy R.R. 1992. "The Evolution of Hearing in Insects as an Adaptation to Predation by Bats." In: *The Evolutionary Biology of Hearing.* eds. D.B. Webster, R.R. Fay, & A.N. Popper.115–129. New York: Springer.

Kristensen, N.P., M.J. Scoble & O. Karscholt. 2007. "Lepidoptera phylogeny and systematics: the state of inventorying moth and butterfly diversity." Zootaxa, 1668: 699–747.

Kritsky, G. 1991. "Darwin's Madagascan Hawkmoth Prediction." *American Entomologist.* Vol: 37, Issue 4, 206–210

Larsen, T. 1992. *The Butterflies of Kenya and Their Natural History.* New York: Oxford University Press

Larsen, T. 1993. "Butterfly Mass Transit." *Natural History.* Vol: 102, Issue 6

National Audubon Society 1981. *Field Guide to Butterflies: North America.* New York: Alfred A. Knopf

Opler, Paul A., Kelly Lotts, and Thomas Naberhaus, coordinators. 2010. Butterflies and Moths of North America. Bozeman, MT: Big Sky Institute. http://www.butterfliesandmoths.org/ Accessed March 15, 2010.

Rubinoff, D. & Haines, W.P. 2005. "Web-Spinning Caterpillar Stalks Snails." *Science*: 309:575

Salmon, M.A. 2000. *The Aurelian Legacy: British Butterflies and Their Collectors.* Berkeley and Los Angeles: University of California Press

Schappert, P. 2000. *A World for Butterflies: Their Lives, Behavior and Future.* Buffalo, NY: Firefly Books

Scoble, M.J. 1992. *The Lepidoptera: Form, Function and Diversity.* London: Oxford University Press

Scott, J.A. 1986. *The Butterflies of North America: A Natural History and Field Guide.* Palo Alto, California: Stanford University Press.

Woodhall, S. 2005. *Field Guide to Butterflies of South Africa.* Cape Town: Struik

Wagner, D.L. 2005. *Princeton Field Guide to Caterpillars of Eastern North America.* New Jersey: Princeton University Press.

PHOTO CREDITS

Index

Acknowledgments

Many thanks to Dr. James Miller for much sound advice and help in shaping the initial idea. At the American Museum of Natural History, I would like to thank David Harvey, Senior Vice President for Exhibition; the staff of the Business Development Department for their advice and support; and the staff of Living Exhibits for offering their favorites for consideration. Special thanks are due to Suzanne Rab Green and Steve Fratello for their suggestions on species selection and help locating them in the vast museum collection, and to Steve Thurston for his work on the scales photograph.

I am very grateful to Pamela Horn, Katherine Furman, Ashley Prine, and Bonnie Naugle of Sterling Publishing for their wonderful ideas, their encouragement, and for keeping me on track.

To Dan Dunwoody of Butterfly Dan's, I am very appreciative for the tour of the farm and for accommodating the photo shoot.

And heartfelt gratitude to my husband, Andrew, for constant encouragement.